The Ultimate Self-Teaching Method!

Play Alto Sax Today!

T0088576

A Complete Guide to the Basics

PLAYBACK+
Speed • Pitch • Balance • Loop

To access audio and video visit:
www.halleonard.com/mylibrary

Enter Code
2042-7623-9097-2127

ISBN 978-1-5400-5242-1

Copyright © 2001, 2003 by HAL LEONARD CORPORATION
International Copyright Secured All Rights Reserved

Visit Hal Leonard Online at
www.halleonard.com

Contact us:
Hal Leonard
7777 West Bluemound Road
Milwaukee, WI 53213
Email: info@halleonard.com

In Europe, contact:
Hal Leonard Europe Limited
42 Wigmore Street
Marylebone, London, W1U 2RN
Email: info@halleonardeurope.com

In Australia, contact:
Hal Leonard Australia Pty. Ltd.
4 Lentara Court
Cheltenham, Victoria, 3192 Australia
Email: info@halleonard.com.au

Introduction

Welcome to *Play Alto Sax Today!*—the series designed to prepare you for any style of saxophone playing, from rock to blues to jazz to country. Whatever your taste in music, *Play Alto Sax Today!* will give you the start you need.

About the Audio & Video

It's easy and fun to play saxophone, and the accompanying audio will make your learning even more enjoyable, as we take you step by step through each lesson and play each song along with a full band. Much like with a real lesson, the best way to learn this material is to read and practice a while first on your own, then listen to the audio. With *Play Alto Sax Today!*, you can learn at your own pace. If there is ever something that you don't quite understand the first time through, go back to the track and listen again. Every musical track has been given a track number, so if you want to practice a song again, you can find it right away.

Some topics in the book include video lessons, so you can see and hear the material being taught. Audio and video are indicated with icons.

Audio Icon   Video Icon

Contents

The Basics

The Parts of the Saxophone ▶

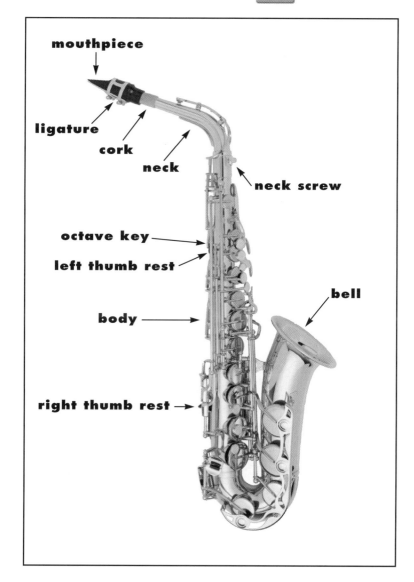

mouthpiece

ligature

cork

neck

neck screw

octave key

left thumb rest

body

bell

right thumb rest

Posture

Whether sitting on the edge of your chair or standing, you should always keep your:

- Spine straight and tall,
- Shoulders back and relaxed, and
- Feet flat on the floor.

Breathing & Air Stream ▶

Breathing is a natural thing we all do constantly, but you must control your breathing while playing the sax. To discover the correct air stream to play your alto sax:

- Place the palm of your hand near your mouth.
- Inhale deeply through the corners of your mouth, keeping your shoulders steady. Your waist should expand like a balloon.
- Whisper "too" as you gradually exhale a stream of air into your palm.

The air you feel is the air stream. It produces sound through the instrument. Your tongue is like a faucet or valve that releases or stops the air stream.

Your First Tone

Your mouth's position on the instrument is called the embouchure *(ahm' bah shure)*. Developing a good embouchure takes time and effort, so carefully follow these beginning steps:

- First place the reed on the mouthpiece.

  Put the thin end of the reed in your mouth to moisten it thoroughly.

  Looking at the flat side of the mouthpiece, the ligature screws extend to your right. Slide the ligature up with your thumb.

  Place the flat side of the moist reed against the opening on the flat side of the mouthpiece. The thin tip of the reed should be almost even with the tip of the mouthpiece (only a hairline of the mouthpiece should be seen above the reed).

  While holding the reed in place with your left thumb, guide the ligature down over the mouthpiece and reed. (If your mouthpiece has two thin lines or grooves around it, position the ligature between these lines.)

  Gently tighten the screws on the ligature.

- Moisten your lips and roll the lower lip over your bottom teeth. About half of the red part of the lower lip should be over the teeth.

- Place the mouthpiece about ½ inch into your mouth with the reed on your lower lip.

- Close your mouth around the mouthpiece like a rubber band. Your upper teeth rest on the top of the mouthpiece and your bottom teeth should gently apply pressure into your bottom lip so that your mouthpiece is being held securely in place.

- The tip of your tongue should be behind your bottom teeth.

- Gently press your tongue forward, but keep the tip behind your bottom teeth. As you do this you will feel the reed touch your tongue about 1/2 inch back from the tip of the tongue so that no air could escape if you were to blow.

- Simultaneously blow into your instrument as you quickly pull your tongue back from the reed as if whispering "too."

- Keep your air moving at a steady rate of speed, and don't allow your cheeks to puff out as you blow.

- This procedure for beginning a note is called "tonguing," and every note that you play should begin this way for the time being.

Reading Music

Musical sounds are indicated by symbols called **notes** written on a **staff**. Notes come in several forms, but every note indicates **pitch** and **rhythm**.

The Staff

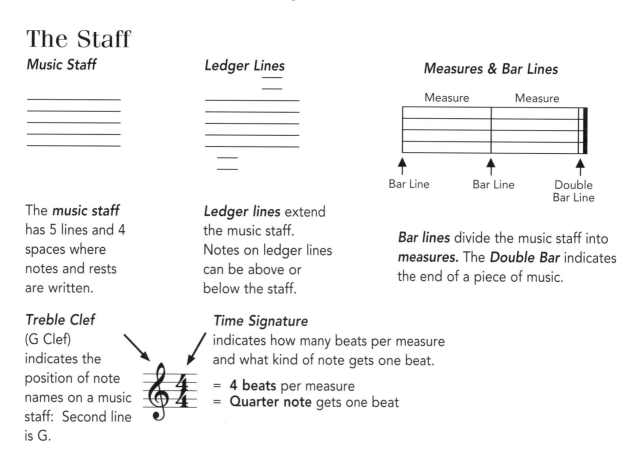

Music Staff

Ledger Lines

Measures & Bar Lines

Measure   Measure

Bar Line   Bar Line   Double Bar Line

The **music staff** has 5 lines and 4 spaces where notes and rests are written.

Ledger lines extend the music staff. Notes on ledger lines can be above or below the staff.

Bar lines divide the music staff into **measures.** The **Double Bar** indicates the end of a piece of music.

Treble Clef (G Clef) indicates the position of note names on a music staff: Second line is G.

Time Signature indicates how many beats per measure and what kind of note gets one beat.

= **4 beats** per measure
= **Quarter note** gets one beat

Pitch

Pitch (the highness or lowness of a note) is indicated by the horizontal placement of the note on the staff. Notes higher on the staff are higher in pitch; notes lower on the staff are lower in pitch. To name the pitches, we use the first seven letters of the alphabet: A, B, C, D, E, F, and G. The **treble clef** (𝄞) assigns a particular pitch name to each line and space on the staff, centered around the pitch G, located on the second line of the staff. Music for the alto sax is always written in the treble clef. (Some instruments may make use of other clefs, which make the lines and spaces represent different pitches.)

Note Names

Each note is on a line or space of the staff. These note names are indicated by the Treble Clef.

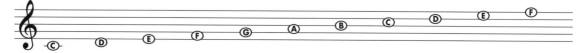

Sharps, Flats, and Naturals

These musical symbols are called accidentals which raise or lower the pitch of a note.

Sharp   ♯   raises the note and remains in effect for the entire measure.

Flat   ♭   lowers the note and remains in effect for the entire measure.

Natural   ♮   cancels a flat (♭) or sharp (♯) and remains in effect for the entire measure.

Rhythm

Rhythm refers to how long, or for how many **beats** a note lasts. The beat is the pulse of music, and like your heartbeat it usually remains very steady. To help keep track of the beats in a piece of music, the staff is divided into **measures**. The **time signature** (numbers such as $\frac{4}{4}$ or $\frac{6}{8}$ at the beginning of the staff) indicates how many beats you will find in each measure. Counting the beats or tapping your foot can help to maintain a steady beat. Tap your foot down on each beat and up on each "&."

$\frac{4}{4}$ Time

Count:	1	&	2	&	3	&	4	&
Tap:	↓	↑	↓	↑	↓	↑	↓	↑

$\frac{4}{4}$ is probably the most common time signature. The **top number** tells you how many beats are in each measure; the **bottom number** tells you what kind of note receives one beat. In $\frac{4}{4}$ time there are four beats in the measure and a **quarter note** (♩ or ♪) equals one beat.

> **4** = **4 beats** per measure
> **4** = **Quarter note** gets one beat

Assembling Your Alto Sax ▶

- Put the thin end of the reed into your mouth to moisten it thoroughly while assembling your instrument. Occasionally rub a small amount of cork grease into the strip of cork around the neck, then wipe the excess off your fingers.

- Hold the body of the sax in your left hand. Many saxophones come with an "end plug" that covers small end of the body of the sax. Take it out and put it aside. You will want to put it back in when you put the instrument away.

- With your right hand, gently twist the neck into the body. Be careful not too squeeze any of the keys tightly or you might bend them. Tighten the neck screw.

- Carefully twist the mouthpiece on the neck so that approximately 1/2 of the cork remains uncovered. Place the reed on the mouthpiece (see "Your First Tone" on page 4).

- Place the neck strap around your neck and attach the hook at the end of the strap to the ring on the back of the sax. Be sure to shorten the strap enough that you can put the mouthpiece into your mouth without having to reach for it.

How to Hold Your Alto Sax

- Place your right thumb under the right thumb rest. This thumb rest should touch your thumb at a point between the knuckle and the thumb nail. Put your left thumb diagonally across the left thumb rest, which looks like a pearl button. Your left thumb should remain on this button at all times.

- The neck strap should support the weight of the instrument. Your thumbs balance the sax so that it stays in the correct position.

- Letting your fingers curve naturally, let the pads of your fingers rest on the keys.

- Hold your instrument as shown:

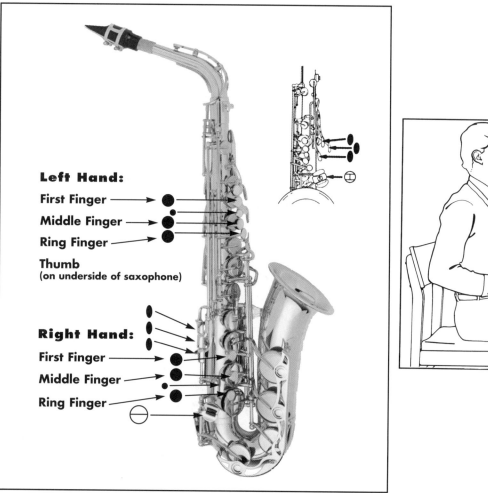

Left Hand:

First Finger

Middle Finger

Ring Finger

Thumb
(on underside of saxophone)

Right Hand:

First Finger

Middle Finger

Ring Finger

Putting Away Your Instrument

- Remove the reed, wipe off excess moisture and return it to the reed case.

- Remove the mouthpiece and wipe the inside with a clean cloth. Once a week, wash the mouthpiece with warm tap water and dry thoroughly.

- Loosen the neck screw, remove the neck and shake out excess moisture. Dry it with the neck cleaner.

- Drop the weight of the chamois or cotton swab into the bell. Pull the swab through the body several times. Replace the end cap and return the instrument to its case.

Track 1

The First Note: D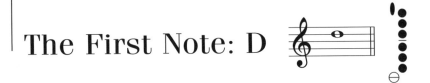

To play "D", place your fingers on the keys as shown. The keys that are colored in should be pressed down.

Notes and Rests

Music uses symbols to indicated both the length of sound and of silence. Symbols indicating sound are called **Notes**. Symbols indicating silence are called **Rests**.

Whole Note/Whole Rest

A whole note means to play for four full beats (a complete measure in $\frac{4}{4}$ time). A whole rest means to be silent for four full beats.

Whole note	Half note	Quarter note	Eighth note
𝅝	𝅗𝅥	♩	♪
Whole rest	Half rest	Quarter rest	Eighth rest
▬	▬	𝄽	𝄾

Listen to the recorded track, then play along. Try to match the sound on the recording.

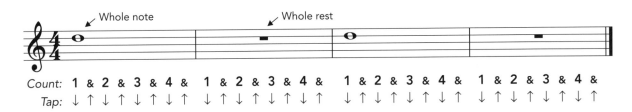

Count: **1** & **2** & **3** & **4** &   **1** & **2** & **3** & **4** &   **1** & **2** & **3** & **4** &   **1** & **2** & **3** & **4** &

Tap: ↓ ↑ ↓ ↑ ↓ ↑ ↓ ↑   ↓ ↑ ↓ ↑ ↓ ↑ ↓ ↑   ↓ ↑ ↓ ↑ ↓ ↑ ↓ ↑   ↓ ↑ ↓ ↑ ↓ ↑ ↓ ↑

Count and Play

Notes and Rests

Quarter Note/Quarter Rest

A quarter note means to play for one full beat. A quarter rest means to be silent for one full beat. There are four quarter notes or quarter rests in a $\frac{4}{4}$ measure.

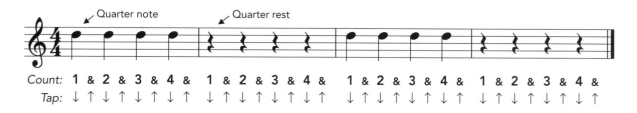

Each note should begin with a quick "tu" to help separate it from the others.

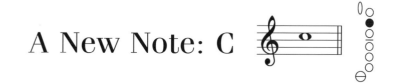

Count: **1** & **2** & **3** & **4** &   **1** & **2** & **3** & **4** &   **1** & **2** & **3** & **4** &   **1** & **2** & **3** & **4** &
Tap: ↓ ↑ ↓ ↑ ↓ ↑ ↓ ↑   ↓ ↑ ↓ ↑ ↓ ↑ ↓ ↑   ↓ ↑ ↓ ↑ ↓ ↑ ↓ ↑   ↓ ↑ ↓ ↑ ↓ ↑ ↓ ↑

Don't just let the track play on. Repeat each exercise until you feel comfortable playing it by yourself and with the audio.

A New Note: C

Look for the fingering diagram next to each new note. Practicing long tones like this will help to develop your sound and your breath control, so don't just move on to the next exercise. Repeat each one several times.

Count/ **1** & **2** & **3** & **4** &   **1** & **2** & **3** & **4** &   **1** & **2** & **3** & **4** &   **1** & **2** & **3** & **4** &
Tap:

Two's A Team

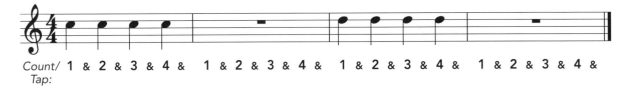

Count/ **1 & 2 & 3 & 4 &**   **1 & 2 & 3 & 4 &**   **1 & 2 & 3 & 4 &**   **1 & 2 & 3 & 4 &**
Tap:

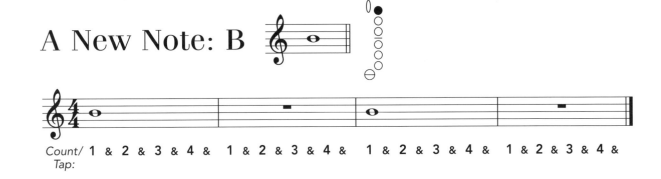

Remember: Rests are silence in music where you play nothing at all. Rests are like notes in that they have their own rhythmic values, instructing you how long (or for how many beats) to pause. Here, four beats of rest can be simplified as a whole rest.

A New Note: B

Count/ **1 & 2 & 3 & 4 &**   **1 & 2 & 3 & 4 &**   **1 & 2 & 3 & 4 &**   **1 & 2 & 3 & 4 &**
Tap:

Keeping Time

To keep a steady tempo, try tapping your foot and counting along with each song. In $\frac{4}{4}$ time, tap your foot four times in each measure and count, "1 & 2 & 3 & 4 &." Your foot should touch the floor on the number and come up on the "&." Each number and each "&" should be exactly the same duration, like the ticking of a clock.

Moving On Up

If your embouchure becomes tired, you can still practice by fingering the notes on your instrument and singing the pitches or counting the rhythm out loud.

Count/ **1 & 2 & 3 & 4 &**   **1 & 2 & 3 & 4 &**   **1 & 2 & 3 & 4 &**   **1 & 2 & 3 & 4 &**
Tap:

Track 7

A New Note: A

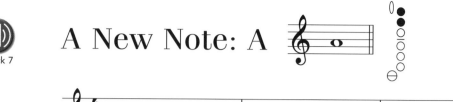

Count/
Tap: 1 & 2 & 3 & 4 &   1 & 2 & 3 & 4 &   1 & 2 & 3 & 4 &   1 & 2 & 3 & 4 &

Track 8

Four By Four

Repeat Signs

Repeat signs ‖: :‖ tell you to repeat everything between them. If only the sign on the right appears (:‖), repeat from the beginning of the piece.

Repeat sign

Count/
Tap: 1 & 2 & 3 & 4 &   1 & 2 & 3 & 4 &   1 & 2 & 3 & 4 &   1 & 2 & 3 & 4 &

Track 9

A New Note: G

Count/
Tap: 1 & 2 & 3 & 4 &   1 & 2 & 3 & 4 &   1 & 2 & 3 & 4 &   1 & 2 & 3 & 4 &

Track 10

The Fab Five

1 & 2 & 3 & 4 &   1 & 2 & 3 & 4 &   1 & 2 & 3 & 4 &   1 & 2 & 3 & 4 &

First Flight

Keep the beat steady by silently counting or tapping while you play.

Rolling Along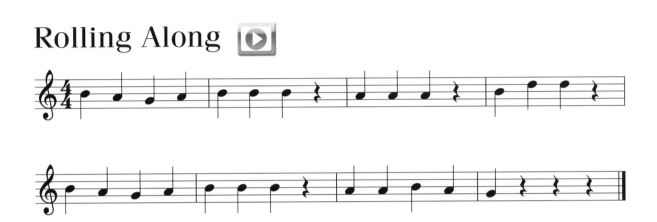

Tonguing

To start each note, whisper the syllable "too." Keep the air stream going continuously. If the notes change, be sure to move your fingers quickly so that each note will come out cleanly. When you come to a rest or the end of the song, just stop blowing. Using your tongue to stop the air will cause an abrupt and unpleasant ending of the sound.

- Play long tones to warm up at the beginning of every practice session.
- Tap, count out loud and sing through each exercise with the audio before you play it.
- Play each exercise several times until you feel comfortable with it.

Track 13

Hot Cross Buns

Notes and Rests

Half Note/Half Rest

A half note means to play for two full beats. (It's equal in length to two quarter notes.) A half rest means to be silent for two beats. There are two half notes or half rests in a $\frac{4}{4}$ measure.

Whole note	Half note	Quarter note	Eighth note
o	♩	♩	♪
Whole rest	Half rest	Quarter rest	Eighth rest

Track 14

Go Tell Aunt Rhodie

Breath Mark

The breath mark (ʼ) indicates a specific place to inhale. Play the proceeding note for the full length then take a deep, quick breath through your mouth.

Remember to let your upper teeth rest on the topside of the mouthpiece! Make certain that your cheeks don't puff out when you blow.

Track 15

The Whole Thing

Remember: a whole rest (-) indicates a whole measure of silence. Note that the whole rest hangs down from the 4th line, whereas the half rest sits on the 3rd line.

Track 16

March Steps

Key Signature – G

A *key signature* (the group of sharps or flats before the time signature) tells which notes are played as sharps or flats throughout the entire piece. In this exercise, all the F's are played as F♯. [This is called the *Key of G*.]

Track 17

Lightly Row

Always be sure to check the key signature before starting a new song.

Reaching Higher (New Note: E)

Fermata

The fermata (⌢) indicates that a note or rest is held somewhat longer than normal.

Fermata

Au Claire De La Lune

Twinkle, Twinkle Little Star

- Keep your reed thoroughly moist, even the part that is against the mouthpiece.
- Keep your thumbs in the correct position at all times and your fingers resting lightly on the pearls of the keys.
- Keep your chin pointed downward and your throat open and free from tension.

Track 21

Deep Pockets (New Note: F♯)

Always practice long tones on each new note.

F♯ (F-sharp)

Track 22

Doodle All Day

Breath Support

In order to play in tune and with a full, beautiful tone, it is necessary to breathe properly and control the air as you play. Quickly take the breath in through your mouth all the way to the bottom of your lungs. Then tighten your stomach muscles and push the air quickly through the alto sax, controlling the air with your lips. Practice this by forming your lips as you do when you play and then blowing against your hand. If the air is cool, you are doing it correctly. If the air is warm, tighten the lips and make the air stream smaller. Keep the air stream moving fast at all times, especially as you begin to run out of air. Practice blowing against your hand and see how long you can keep the air going. Work to keep the air stream from beginning to end.

Now try this with your alto sax. Select a note that is comfortable to play and see how long you can hold it. Listen carefully to yourself to see if the tone gets louder or softer, changes pitch slightly, or if the quality of the tone changes. Do this a few times every time you practice, trying to hold the note a little longer each time and maintain a good sound.

Jingle Bells

Dynamics

Dynamics refer to how loud or soft the music is. Traditionally, many musical terms (including dynamic markings) are called by their Italian names:

f	forte *(four' tay)*	loud
mf	mezzo forte *(met' zoh four' tay)*	moderately loud
p	piano *(pee ahn' oh)*	soft

Producing a louder sound requires more air, but you should use full breath support at all dynamic levels.

My Dreydl

Pick-up Notes

Sometimes there are notes that come before the first full measure. They are called *pick-up notes*. Often, when a song begins with a pick-up measure, the note's value (in beats) is subtracted from the last measure. To play this song with a one beat pick-up, you count "1, 2, 3" and start playing on beat 4.

Last measure has 3 beats, not 4

Eighth Note Jam

Notes and Rests

Eighth Note/Eighth Rest

An eighth note half the value of a quarter note, that is, half a beat. A eighth rest means to be silent for half a beat. There are eight eighth notes or eight eighth rests in a $\frac{4}{4}$ measure.

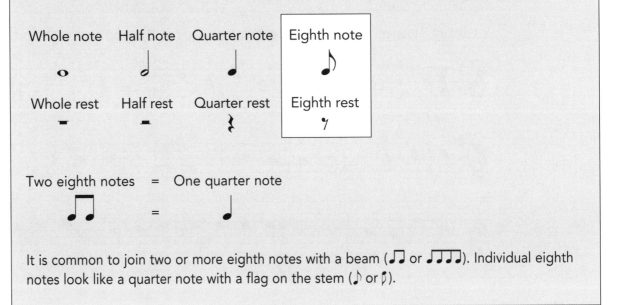

It is common to join two or more eighth notes with a beam (♫ or ♫♫). Individual eighth notes look like a quarter note with a flag on the stem (♪ or ♪).

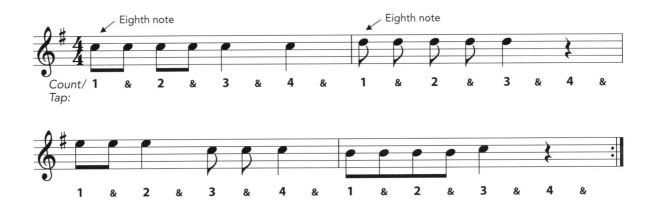

Eighth Note Counting

The first eighth note comes on "1" as your foot taps the floor. The second happens as your foot moves up on "&." The third is on "2" and the fourth is on the next "&" and so forth. Remember to count and tap in a steady and even manner, like the ticking of a clock.

Skip To My Lou

Keep your fingers resting lightly on the keys and curved comfortably.

Long, Long Ago

Track 27

Good posture will improve your sound.

Oh, Susanna

Track 28

Notice the pick-up notes.

William Tell

Track 29

19

- Use plenty of air and keep it moving *through* the saxophone. Blow enough air through the instrument to get a full tone. Compare your tone to the recording.

- Let your body support the weight of the instrument with the neck strap. Don't try to lift the sax with your right thumb. Your thumbs should *balance* the sax.

Track 30

Two By Two

> ### $\frac{2}{4}$ Time
>
> A time signature of $\frac{2}{4}$ means that a quarter note gets one beat, but there are only two beats in a measure.

Count/ Tap: 1 & 2 & 1 & 2 & 1 & 2 & 1 & 2 &

1 & 2 & 1 & 2 & 1 & 2 & 1 & 2 &

Track 31

High School Cadets March

> ## Tempo Markings
>
> The speed or pace of music is called **tempo**. Tempo markings are usually written above the staff. Many of these terms come from the Italian.
>
> | | | |
> |---|---|---|
> | **Allegro** | *(ah lay' grow)* | Fast tempo |
> | **Moderato** | *(mah der ah' tow)* | Medium or moderate tempo |
> | **Andante** | *(ahn dahn' tay)* | Slower "walking" tempo |

Hey, Ho! Nobody's Home
(New Note: E)

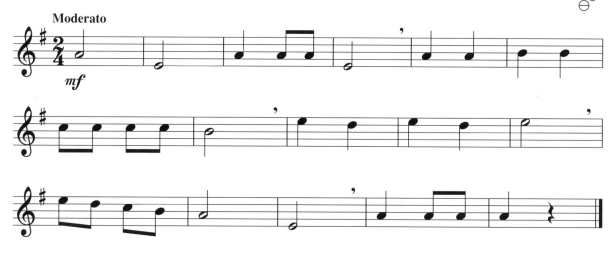

Octaves

Notes that have the same name but are eight notes higher or lower are called **octaves**. You already knew how to play an E, but this new E is one octave lower. When using the "octave key" with your left thumb, just roll the left edge of your thumb onto the octave key. Make sure your thumb is still partially on the pearl thumb button. Practice playing both E's one after the other like this:

The lower notes will be played more easily if you loosen your throat and relax your lips slightly.

Play The Dynamics

Dynamics

Gradual changes in volume are indicated by these symbols:

< **Crescendo** (gradually louder) sometimes abbreviated *cresc.*

> **Decrescendo** or **Diminuendo** (gradually softer) sometimes abbreviated *dim.*

Remember to keep the air stream moving fast both as you get louder by gradually using more air on the crescendo, *and* as you get softer by gradually using less air on the decrescendo.

Aura Lee

Frère Jacques

Hard Rock Blues

Posture

Good body posture will allow you to take in a full, deep breath and control the air better as you play. Sit or stand with your spine straight and tall. Your shoulders should be back and relaxed. Think about your posture as you begin playing and check it several times while playing.

Track 37

Alouette

Tie

A *tie* is a curved line connecting two notes of the same pitch. It indicates that instead of playing both notes, you play the first note and hold it for the total time value of both notes.

 = 2 beats

Dot

A *dot* adds half the value of the note to which it is attached. A dotted half note (♩.) has a total time value of three beats:

Dotted half note (three beats) = Half note (two beats) + Quarter note (one beat)

Therefore, a dotted half note has exactly the same value as a half note tied to a quarter note. Playing track 37 again, compare this music to the previous example:

New Directions (New Note: D)

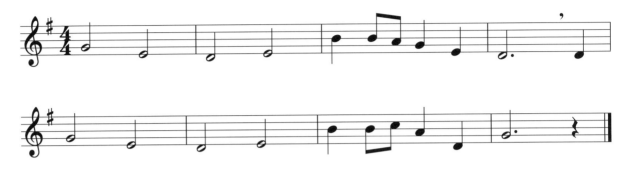

This D is an octave lower than the D you already know. Once again, practice going from one D to the other. Your left thumb should just roll slightly onto the octave key, just enough to open it when needed.

The Nobles

Ties are useful when you need to extend the value of a note across a bar line. Notice the tie across the bar line between the first and second measure. The D on the third beat is held through the following beats 4 and 1.

Three Beat Jam

¾ Time

The next song is in ¾ time signature. That is, three beats (quarter notes) per measure.

Three beats per measure

Quarter note gets one beat

Count: **1** & **2** & **3** & **1** & **2** & **3** & **1** & **2** & **3** & **1** & **2** & **3** &

¾ time feels very different from 4/4 time. Putting more emphasis on the first beat of each measure will help you feel the new meter.

Morning (from Peer Gynt)

Andante

p

mf   *p*

Hand and Finger Position

Now is a good time to go back to page 7 and review proper hand and finger position. This is very important to proper technique. Keeping the fingers curved and close to their assigned keys will allow your fingers and hands to be relaxed and will aid in getting from one note to another quickly, easily, and accurately. The further you lift your fingers off the keys, the more likely that you will put them down on the wrong key or not securely close the key. Besides that, fingers pointing in all directions doesn't look good!

- As you finger the notes on your sax, you can practice quietly by speaking the names of the notes, counting out the rhythms, or singing or whistling the pitches.
- Don't let your cheeks puff out when you play.

Track 42

Mexican Clapping Song ("Chiapanecas")

Accent

The accent (>) means you should emphasize the note to which it is attached. Do this by using a more explosive "t" on the "tu" with which you produce the note.

Track 43

Hot Muffins (New Note: F)

Sharps, Flats, and Naturals

Any sharp (♯), flat (♭), or natural (♮) sign that appears in the music but is not in the key signature is called an **accidental**. The accidental in the next example is F♮ and it effects all of the F's for the rest of the measure.

A **sharp** (♯) raises the pitch of a note by one half step.
A **flat** (♭) lowers the pitch of a note by one half step.
A **natural** (♮) cancels a previous sharp or flat, returning a note to its original pitch.

When a song requires a note to be a half step higher or lower, you'll see a sharp (♯), flat (♭), or natural (♮) sign in front of it. This tells you to raise or lower the note *for that measure only*. We'll see more of these "accidentals" as we continue learning more notes on the sax.

Natural sign

Play all F's in this measure as F♮ (F-naturals).

Cossack Dance

Notice the repeat sign at the end of the fourth measure. Although this particular repeat sign does not occur at the end of the exercise, it behaves just like any other repeat sign. Play the repeated section twice, then continue.

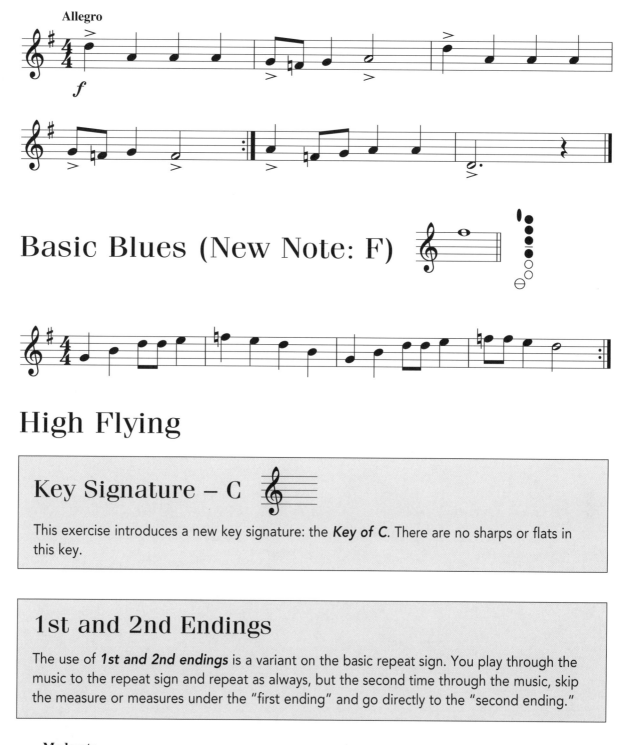

Basic Blues (New Note: F)

High Flying

Key Signature – C

This exercise introduces a new key signature: the **Key of C**. There are no sharps or flats in this key.

1st and 2nd Endings

The use of **1st and 2nd endings** is a variant on the basic repeat sign. You play through the music to the repeat sign and repeat as always, but the second time through the music, skip the measure or measures under the "first ending" and go directly to the "second ending."

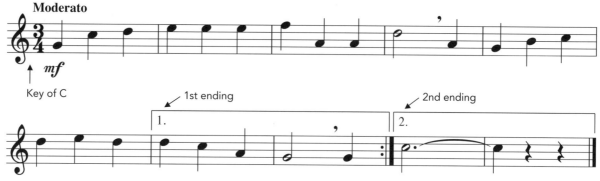

Up On A Housetop

Always check the key signature before you play.

The Big Airstream (New Note: G)

Track 48

Waltz Theme

Track 49

Moderato

Down By The Station

Track 50

Allegro

Banana Boat Song

D.C. al Fine

At the **D.C. al Fine**, play again from the beginning, stopping at **Fine**. D.C. is the abbreviation for Da Capo *(dah cah' poh)*, which means "to the beginning." Fine *(fee' neh)* means "the end."

Track 52

Razor's Edge (New Note: C♯)

On the saxophone, this C♯ is played "open," that is, no keys are pressed.

Sharp Sign

A sharp sign (♯) raises the pitch of a note by a half-step for the remainder of the measure.

Track 53

The Music Box

Track 54

Smooth Operator

Slur

A curved line connecting notes of different pitch is called a *slur*. Notice the difference between a slur and a tie, which connects notes of the *same* pitch.

Only tongue the first note of a slur. As you finger the next note, keep the breath going. You must precisely change the fingering from one note to the next to prevent extraneous pitches from sounding.

Track 55

Gliding Along

This exercise is almost identical to the previous one. Notice how the different slurs change the tonguing.

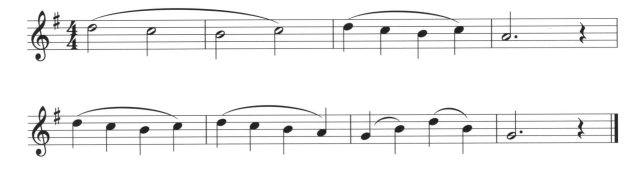

Track 56

Take The Lead (New Note: F♯)

Remember to practice the octaves when you learn a new note.

Track 57

The Cold Wind

Phrase

A phrase is a musical "sentence," often 2 or 4 measures long. Try to play a phrase in one breath.

32

Satin Latin

Key Signature – D

A key signature with two sharps indicates that all written F's and C's should be played as F♯'s and C♯'s. This is the **Key of D**.

Multiple Measure Rest

Sometimes you won't play for several measures. The number above the **multiple measure rest** (▬) indicates how many full measures to rest. Count through the silent measures.

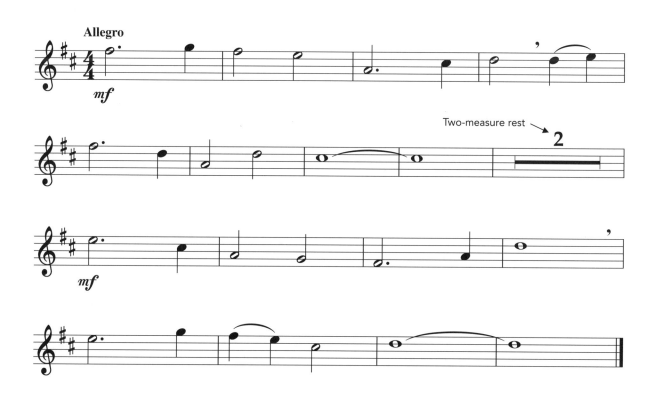

Two-measure rest

March Militaire

Track 59

Allegro

The Flat Zone (New Note: B♭)

Track 60

Flat Sign

A flat sign (♭) lowers the pitch of a note by a half-step for the remainder of the measure.

Learning this note, remember two things. First, keep your fingertips on the pearls of the keys at all times. Second, just turn your right hand inward slightly so that you press down the side B-flat key with the side of your index finger.

Flat sign

On Top Of Old Smokey

Check the key signature.

All Through The Night

Dotted Quarter Note

Remember that a dot adds half the value of the note. A dotted quarter note followed by a eighth note (♩. ♪) and (♩͜♪♪) have the same rhythmic value.

Sea Chanty

Always use a full air stream.

Track 64

Scarborough Fair

Track 65

Auld Lang Syne

- Since the lower tones sometimes tend to be louder, be sure to work for a smooth, even sound throughout your range.

- Play smoothly and evenly by keeping your fingers close to the keys at all times.

Track 66

Crossing Over (New Note: A)

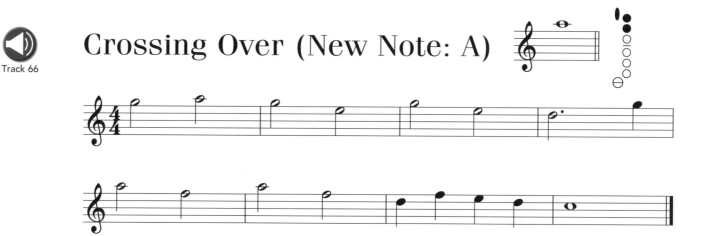

Track 67

Michael Row The Boat Ashore

Repeat the section of music enclosed by the repeat signs (‖: ═ :‖). If 1st and 2nd endings are used, they are played as usual—but go back only to the first repeat sign, not to the beginning.

Botany Bay

Track 68

Track 69

Finlandia

C Time Signature

Common time (C) is the same as $\frac{4}{4}$.

Track 70

When The Saints Go Marching In

Lowland Gorilla Walk
(Alternate fingering: C)

Several notes on the saxophone can be played with more than one fingering. These different fingerings are called "alternate fingerings." When going between this C to the B just below it, it may be easier to use this new fingering.

The Streets of Laredo

A Quick Review

Posture

Whether sitting on the edge of your chair or standing, you should always keep your:

- Spine straight and tall,

- Shoulders back and relaxed, and

- Feet flat on the floor.

Holding Your Saxophone

- The weight of your instrument should be completely supported by the neck strap. Don't try to hold up the sax with your right thumb. Instead, make sure the neck strap is adjusted so the mouthpiece is exactly at the correct height.

- Keep your fingers arched comfortably, close to the keys. Don't move your hands out of position when using the side keys. Your hands should always be relaxed. Tensing up your hands will limit your dexterity and possibly cause physical damage

Taking Care of Your Instrument

- To remove finger marks from your saxophone, wipe the outside of the instrument with a soft, clean cloth.

- After each practice session, pull the neck swab through the saxophone neck.

- If the neck does not twist easily into the body, clean the tenon with a soft, clean cloth.

- Be careful not to brush the end of the reed against anything because the tip of the reed is very thin and is easily damaged.

- After each practice session, remember to pull the swab through each section of your saxophone. Many experienced saxophone players prefer not to pull a swab through their mouthpieces. A tissue works very well and will not cause abrasions which could adversely effect mouthpiece playing quality.

Warm-ups

Like athletes, musicians need to "warm up" before they perform. A good warm-up will loosen up the muscles of the embouchure and tongue, relax the hands, and focus your mind on playing the instrument. The first three tracks are good warm-up exercises that should be played every day. Before each exercise, take a full and comfortable breath. Work for a smooth, steady tone.

Track 73

Range and Flexibility Builder

Track 74

Technique Trax

Roll the tip of your left thumb up to the octave key. Don't lift it and put it back down. Always remember to keep your thumb on the left thumb key.

Track 75

More Technique Trax

- Be certain that your cheeks don't puff out when you blow.

- For good tone, stretch about half of the red part of your lower lip over your teeth and point your chin downward so it feels long and flat. The reed rests on the outer skin of your lower lip while your upper teeth rest on the top side of the mouthpiece.

- Keep your throat open and your tongue relaxed.

- Blow enough air through your saxophone to produce a full, even tone.

Track 76

Eighth Note March

Eighth Note/Rest

Recall that an eighth note (♪ or ♩) gets ½ of one beat. An equivalent period of silence is represented by an *eighth rest* (𝄾).

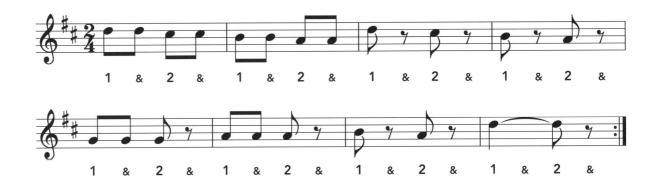

Track 77

Minuet

Track 78

Eighth Notes Off the Beat

Eighth Note Scramble

Track 79

Dancing Melody (New Note: E♭)

Track 80

El Capitan

Allegro

Track 81

Ready for a quick lesson in music theory? A *scale* is a sequence of notes in ascending or descending order. Like a musical "ladder," each step is the next consecutive note in the key. The scale in the key of G is a specific pattern of **half steps** and **whole steps** (more on this later) between one G and another G an *octave* higher or lower.

The same pattern of half steps and whole steps beginning on a different pitch would produce a different key with a different key signature.

The distance between two pitches is called an *interval*. Starting with "1" on the lower note, count each line and space between the notes. The number of the higher note is the distance of the interval. A whole step or half step is called a **second**, the interval between steps 1 and 3 is called a **third**, and so on. Notice that the interval between scale steps 4 and 6, for example, is also a third.

You already know a sharp raises the pitch of a note. Now you know a sharp raises the pitch of a note by a half-step. Similarly, a flat lowers the pitch of a note one half-step. Two notes that are written differently, but sound the same (and are played with the same fingering) are called enharmonics.

Track 82

Dark Shadows – E♭/D♯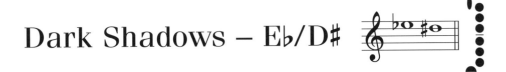

Notice the D♯ in the second full measure (that is, not counting the partial measure with the pick-up note). It is the same pitch and is played with the same fingering as the E♭ in the fourth measure.

Pick-up note

Track 83

Notes in Disguise – B♭/A♯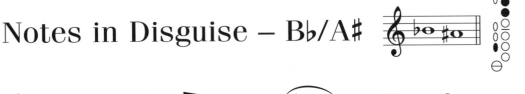

Half-Steppin'
(Alternate Fingering: F♯)

Chromatic Scale

At the beginning of this lesson, we saw examples of half steps and whole steps. The smallest distance between two notes is a half-step. A scale made up of consecutive half-steps is called a **_chromatic scale_**.

Alternate Fingerings

Many notes on the saxophone can be played with more than one fingering. This **_alternate fingering_** for F♯ should be used whenever it precedes or follows an F♮. Try it both ways and you'll see why using the alternate (or, chromatic) fingering is easier.

Alt.

Alt.

March Slav

Largo

Largo (*lahr' goh*) is a tempo indication that means "slow and solemn."

Egyptian Dance

Track 86

Look for the enharmonics.

Chroma-Zone

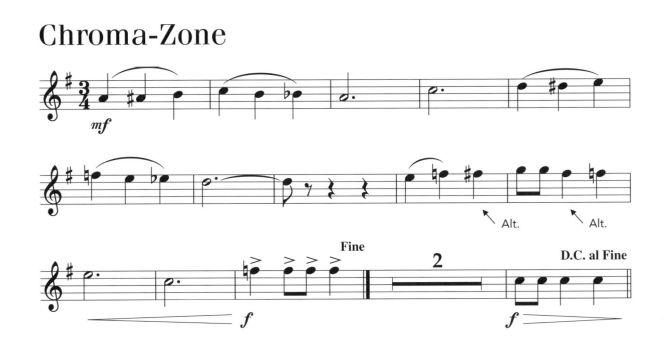

Track 87

- No two reeds are exactly alike. You may have to try several before you find one that plays well for you.

- Your saliva is alkaline and soon will begin to break down the cellular structure of the reed that enables it to vibrate. Some reeds will last much longer than others.

- A good reed will have a full, rich tone and will play equally well in both the high and low registers.

Track 88

Technique Trax

Track 89

Treading Lightly

Staccato

Staccato (*sta kah' toe*) notes are played lightly and with separation. They are marked with a dot above or below the note. Shorten each note by stopping the air stream.

Smooth Move

Tenuto

Tenuto (tih noo' toe) notes are played smoothly and connected, holding each note for its full value until the next is played. They are marked with a straight line above or below the note.

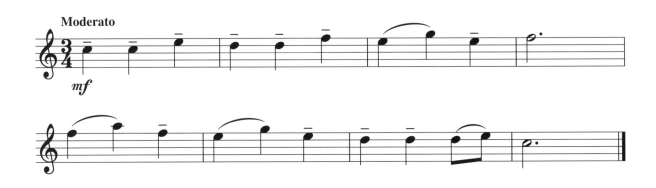

Shifting Gears

Technique Trax

Track 93

Grandfather's Clock

Track 94

Glow Worm

Allegretto, Ritardando

There are two new terms in this exercise. **Allegretto** *(ahl ih gret' toh)* is a tempo indication, usually a little slower than Allegro and with a lighter style. **Ritardando** *(rih tar dahn' doh)* means the tempo gradually gets slower. It is usually abbreviated **rit.** or **ritard**.

Paul Lincke

Track 95

Alma Mater (New Note: B)

Always practice long tones on new notes.

Track 96

Loch Lomond

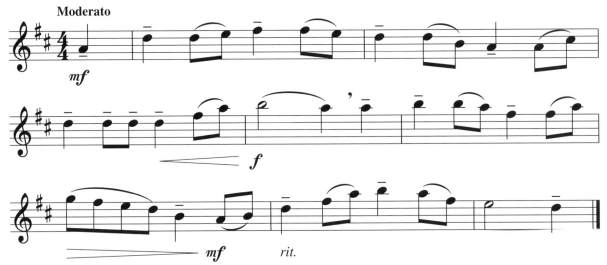

Track 97

Molly Malone

Key Change

The key can change in the middle of a piece. You will usually see a double bar line and a new key signature at the **key change**. You may also see natural signs reminding you to "cancel" previous sharps and flats.

Track 98

A Cut Above

Alla Breve

Alla Breve (ah' la bra' ve), commonly called **cut time**, has a time signature of ¢ or $\frac{2}{2}$. The top "2" indicates two beats per measure. The bottom "2" means a half note (♩), not a quarter note, gets one beat. Of course, this means a whole note (o) receives two beats and a quarter note (♩) only gets ½ beat.

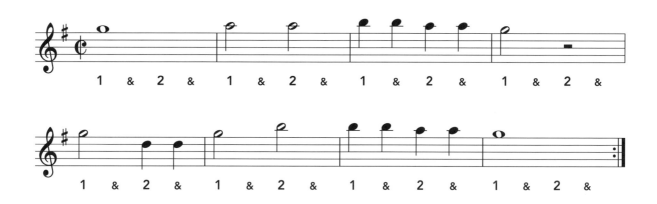

Track 99

Yankee Doodle

First, play the version in $\frac{2}{4}$. Then repeat the track and play the cut time version. Is there any difference?

51

The Victors

Notice the ♩. ♩ patterns. In cut time, the dotted half note receives 1½ beats and the quarter note receives ½ beat.

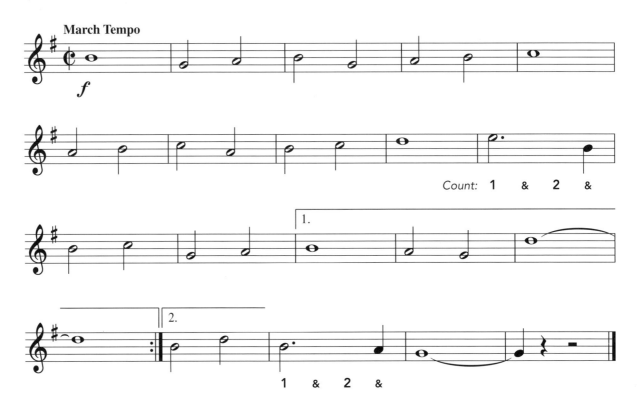

A-Roving

Mezzo Piano

We have already seen dynamic markings such as *p*, *mf*, and *f*. **Mezzo piano**
(*met' zo pee ahn' no*), abbreviated *mp*, means moderately soft: a little louder
than piano, not as loud as mezzo forte.

Remember to use a full breath support at all dynamic levels.

In Sync

Syncopation

Generally, the notes **on** the beat (that's the 1's, 2's, 3's and such) are played a bit stronger
or louder than the notes on the **off-beats** (that's the &'s). When an accent or emphasis is
given to a note that is not normally on a strong beat, it is called **syncopation**. This sort of
"off-beat" feel is common in many popular and classical styles.

La Roca

You're A Grand Old Flag

Rehearsal Numbers

In longer pieces, the publisher sometimes includes **rehearsal numbers** to help the conductor or band leader start and stop the ensemble easily. Sometimes they are letters like A, B, C; sometimes numbers like 1, 2, 3. Frequently, such as here, they are measure numbers.

Crescendo, Decrescendo

A gradual increase in volume is called **crescendo** *(kreh shen' doh)*. It is usually indicated by **cresc.** or ◁. A corresponding gradual decrease in volume is called **decrescendo** *(deh kre shen' do)*, abbreviated **decresc.**, or **diminuendo** *(dih meh nyu ehn' doh)*, abbreviated **dim**. A decrescendo (diminuendo) may be represented by ▷.

George M. Cohan

The Minstrel Boy (New Note: G♯)

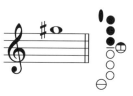

This exercise introduces a new key signature: the key of A. Play all F's as F♯, all C's as C♯, and all G's as G♯.

Close Call (New Note: G♯)

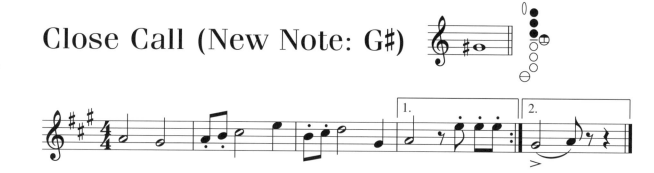

Winning Streak

Pay attention to the syncopation. It is similar to what you played earlier, but now the time signature is ₵.

Sixteenth Note Fanfare

Sixteenth Notes

A sixteenth note (♬ or ♪) has half the value of an eighth note. In $\frac{4}{4}$, $\frac{3}{4}$, or $\frac{2}{4}$ time, four sixteenth notes (♬♬) get one beat.

Moving Along

Comin' Round The Mountain Variations

Sea Chantey

Observe that an eighth note and two sixteenths are normally written ♪♫. This has the same rhythmic pattern as ♫♫.

Track 112

American Fanfare (New Note: B♭)

Maestoso

Maestoso *(mah ee stoh' soh)* means "majestic, stately, and dignified."

Track 113

Scale Study

This new key signature indicates the key of F. The first four measures consist of the F scale.

57

Bill Bailey

Rhythm Etude

Track 115

Observe that two sixteenth notes followed by an eighth are normally written ♫♩. This has the same rhythmic pattern as ♫♫♩.

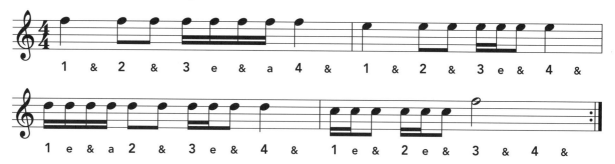

Celtic Dance

Track 116

The Galway Piper

Track 117

Marching Along

Track 118

The figures ♩♫♪ and ♩.♪ are equivalent.

S'vivon

Toreador Song

Track 121

La Cumparsita

(New Note: E♭/D♯)

Track 122

The Yellow Rose Of Texas

Check the key signature.

Scale Study (New Note: C)

American Patrol

Aria (from Marriage of Figaro)

The Stars And Stripes Forever

John Philip Sousa

Track 127

Lazy Day

$\frac{6}{8}$ Time

Now you will be introduced to a new time signature: $\frac{6}{8}$. The "6" on top indicates that there are six beats per measure. The "8" on the bottom indicates that the eighth note gets one beat. If the eighth note (♪) gets one beat, then it follows that a dotted quarter note (♩.) receives three beats and a dotted half note (𝅗𝅥.) gets six.

$\frac{6}{8}$ time is usually played with slight emphasis on the 1st and 4th beats of each measure. This divides the measure into two groups of three beats each.

1 2 3 4 5 6   1 2 3 4 5 6   1 2 3 4 5 6   1 2 3 4 5 6

Track 128

Row Your Boat

Andante

mf

Track 129

Jolly Good Fellow

Moderato

f   Pick-up on beat 6

When Johnny Comes Marching Home

In faster music, the primary beats in $\frac{6}{8}$ time (beats 1 and 4) will make the music feel like it's counted in "2," but with a **triple subdivision** of the beat rather than **duple**.

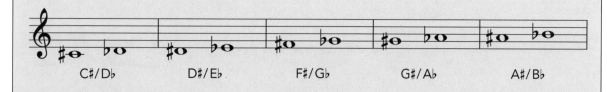

Enharmonics

Remember that notes which sound the same but have different names are called **enharmonics**. These are some common enharmonics that you'll use in the exercises below.

C#/Db   D#/Eb   F#/Gb   G#/Ab   A#/Bb

Chromatic passages are usually written using enharmonic notes – sharps when going up and flats when going down.

Track 131

Chromatic Scale

Practice slowly until you are sure of all the fingerings.

F# Alt.

Gb Alt.

Technique Trax

Track 132

Habañera (from Carmen)

Track 133

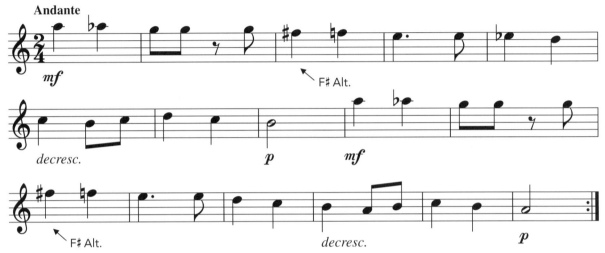

Andante

mf

F♯ Alt.

decresc.   *p*   *mf*

F♯ Alt.   *decresc.*   *p*

Chromatic Crescendo

Track 134

Moderato

p   *cresc.*

F♯ Alt.   F♯ Alt.

mf ──────────── *f*   G♭ Alt.   *rall.*

Staccato Study

Track 135

Moderato

p   *cresc.*

f   *decresc.*   *p*

Track 136

Yankee Doodle Dandy

George M. Cohan

Three To Get Ready

Track 137

> ### Triplet
>
> A *triplet* is a group of 3 notes played in the time usually occupied by 2. In $\frac{2}{4}$, $\frac{3}{4}$, or $\frac{4}{4}$ time, an eighth note triplet () is spread evenly across one beat.

Triplet Study

Track 138

Theme From Faust

Track 139

Scale Study

New Notes: C# D

Over The River And Through The Woods

On The Move

Track 143

Higher Ground

Track 144

Doodle All Day

Track 145

D.S. March

D.S. al Fine

Play until you see **D.S. al Fine**. Then go back to the sign (𝄋) and play until the word *Fine*.
D.S. is the abbreviation for **Dal Segno** *(dahl say' nio)*, which is Italian for "from the sign," and
Fine *(fee' nay)* means "the end."

Tarantella

Emperor Waltz

Andantino

Andantino (ahn dahn tee' noh) is a tempo between Andante and Moderato.

Unfinished Symphony Theme

Legato

Legato (leh gah' toh) means to play in a smooth, graceful manner, almost as if everything was slurred.

Greensleeves

Alto Sax Scales and Arpeggios

Key of G

Alto Sax Scales and Arpeggios

Key of C

1.

2.

3.

4.

Alto Sax Scales and Arpeggios

Key of D

Alto Sax Scales and Arpeggios

Key of F

1.

2.

3.

4.

Alto Sax Scales and Arpeggios

Key of A

1.

2.

3.

4.

Glossary of Musical Terms

Accent	An Accent mark (>) means you should emphasize the note to which it is attached.
Accidental	Any sharp (♯), flat (♭), or natural (♮) sign that appears in the music but is not in the key signature is called an Accidental.
Alla Breve	Commonly called cut time. has a time signature of ¢ or $\frac{2}{2}$.
Allegretto	A tempo indication usually a little slower than Allegro and with a lighter style.
Allegro	Fast tempo.
Andante	Slower "walking" tempo.
Andantino	A tempo between Andante and Moderato.
Arpeggio	An Arpeggio is a "broken" chord whose notes are played individually.
Bass Clef (𝄢)	(F Clef) indicates the position of note names on a music staff: The fourth line in Bass Clef is F.
Bar Lines	Bar Lines divide the music staff into measures.
Beat	The Beat is the pulse of music, and like a heartbeat it should remain very steady. Counting aloud and foot-tapping help maintain a steady beat.
Breath Mark	The Breath Mark (ʼ) indicates a specific place to inhale. Play the proceeding note for the full length then take a deep, quick breath through your mouth.
Chord	When two or more notes are played together, they form a Chord or harmony.
Chromatic Notes	Chromatic Notes are altered with sharps, flats and natural signs which are not in the key signature.
Chromatic Scale	The smallest distance between two notes is a half-step, and a scale made up of consecutive half-steps is called a Chromatic Scale.
Common Time	Common Time (𝄴) is the same as $\frac{4}{4}$ time signature.
Crescendo	Play gradually louder. (*cresc.*)
D.C. al Fine	D.C. al Fine means to play again from the beginning, stopping at Fine. D.C. is the abbreviation for Da Capo, or "to the beginning," and Fine means "the end."
D.S. al Fine	Play until you see D.S. al Fine. Then to back to the sign (𝄋) and play until the word Fine. D.S. is the abbreviation for Dal Segno, which is Italian for 'from the sign," and Fine means "the end."
Decrescendo	Play gradually softer. (*decresc.*)

Glossary continued

Diminuendo	Same as decrescendo. (*dim.*)
Dotted Half Note	A note three beats long in duration (𝅗𝅥.). A dot adds half the value of the note.
Dotted Quarter Note	A note one and a half beats long in duration (♩.). A dot adds half the value of the note.
Double Bar (‖)	Indicates the end of a piece of music.
Duet	A composition with two different parts played together.
Dynamics	Dynamics indicate how loud or soft to play a passage of music. Remember to use full breath support to control your tone at all dynamic levels.
Eighth Note	An Eighth Note (♪) receives half the value of a quarter note, that is, half a beat. Two or more eighth notes are usually joined together with a beam, like this: ♫
Eighth Rest	Indicates 1/2 beat of silence. (𝄾)
Embouchure	Your mouth's position on the mouthpiece of the instrument.
Enharmonics	Two notes that are written differently, but sound the same (and played with the same fingering) are called Enharmonics.
Fermata	The Fermata (𝄐) indicates that a note (or rest) is held somewhat longer than normal.
1st & 2nd Endings	The use of 1st and 2nd Endings is a variant on the basic repeat sign. You play through the music to the repeat sign and repeat as always, but the second time through the music, skip the measure or measures under the "first ending" and go directly to the "second ending."
Flat (♭)	Lowers the note a half step and remains in effect for the entire measure.
Forte (*f*)	Play loudly.
Half Note	A Half Note (𝅗𝅥) receives two beats. It's equal in length to two quarter notes.
Half Rest	The Half Rest (𝄼) marks two beats of silence.
Harmony	Two or more notes played together. Each combination forms a chord.
Interval	The distance between two pitches is an Interval.
Key Change	When a song changes key you usually see a double bar line and the new key signature at the key change. You may also see natural signs reminding you to "cancel" previous sharps and flats.
Key Signature	A Key Signature (the group of sharps or flats before the time signature) tells which notes are played as sharps or flats throughout the entire piece.
Largo	Play very slow.

Ledger Lines	Ledger Lines extend the music staff. Notes on ledger lines can be above or below the staff.
Legato	Legato means to play in a smooth, graceful manner, almost as if everything was slurred.
Mezzo Forte (*mf*)	Play moderately loud.
Mezzo Piano (*mp*)	Play moderately soft.
Moderato	Medium or moderate tempo.
Multiple Measure Rest	The number above the staff tells you how many full measures to rest. Count each measure of rest in sequence. (▬)
Music Staff	The Music Staff has 5 lines and 4 spaces where notes and rests are written.
Natural Sign (♮)	Cancels a flat (♭) or sharp (♯) and remains in effect for the entire measure.
Notes	Notes tell us how high or low to play by their placement on a line or space of the music staff, and how long to play by their shape.
Phrase	A Phrase is a musical "sentence," often 2 or 4 measures long.
Piano (*p*)	Play soft.
Pitch	The highness or lowness of a note which is indicated by the horizontal placement of the note on the music staff.
Pick-Up Notes	One or more notes that come before the first full measure. The beats of Pick-Up Notes are subtracted from the last measure.
Quarter Note	A Quarter Note (♩) receives one beat. There are 4 quarter notes in a $\frac{4}{4}$ measure.
Quarter Rest	The Quarter Rest (𝄽) marks one beat of silence.
Repeat Sign	The Repeat Sign (:‖) means to play once again from the beginning without pause. Repeat the section of music enclosed by the repeat signs (‖:≡:‖). If 1st and 2nd endings are used, they are played as usual—but go back only to the first repeat sign, not to the beginning.
Rests	Rests tell us to count silent beats.
Rhythm	Rhythm refers to how long, or for how many beats a note lasts.
Ritardando (*rit.*)	Means the tempo gradually gets slower.
Scale	A Scale is a sequence of notes in ascending or descending order. Like a musical "ladder," each step is the next consecutive note in the key signature.
Sharp (♯)	Raises the note a half step and remains in effect for the entire measure.

Glossary continued

Sixteenth Note A sixteenth note (♬ or ♪) has half the value of an eighth note. In $\frac{4}{4}$, $\frac{3}{4}$, or $\frac{2}{4}$ time, four sixteenth notes (♬♬) get one beat.

Slur A curved line connecting notes of different pitch is called a Slur.

Staccato Play the notes lightly and with separation.

Tempo Tempo is the speed of music.

Tempo Markings Tempo Markings are usually written above the staff, in Italian. (Allegro, Moderato, Andante)

Tenuto Play the notes smoothly and connected, holding each note for its full value until the next is played

Tie A Tie is a curved line connecting two notes of the same pitch. It indicates that instead of playing both notes, you play the first note and hold it for the total time value of both notes.

Time Signature Indicates how many beats per measure and what kind of note gets one beat.

Treble Clef (𝄞) (G Clef) indicates the position of note names on a music staff: The second line in Treble Clef is G.

Trio A Trio is a composition with three parts played together.

Triplet A triplet is a group of three notes played in the time usually occupied by two. In $\frac{2}{4}$, $\frac{3}{4}$, or $\frac{4}{4}$, time, an eighth note triplet (♪♪♪) is spread evenly across one beat.

Whole Note A Whole Note (𝅝) lasts for four full beats (a complete measure in $\frac{4}{4}$ time).

Whole Rest The Whole Rest (▬) indicates a whole measure of silence.

Fingering Chart for Alto Sax

Fingering Chart for Alto Sax

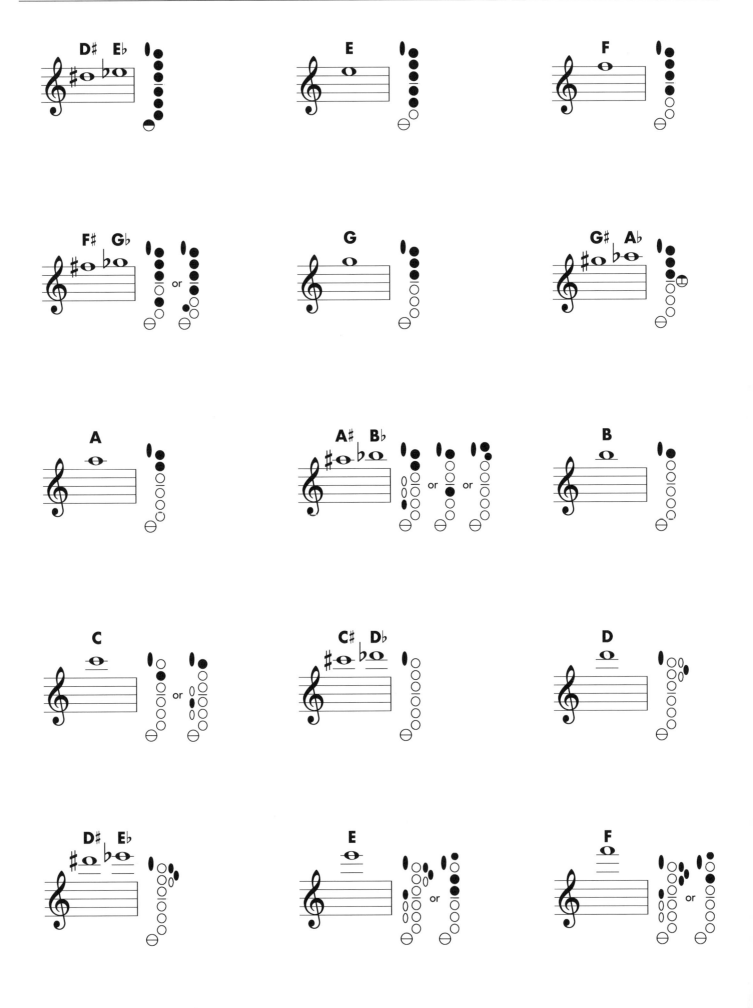

Play Today! Series

The Ultimate Self-Teaching Series

These are complete guides to the basics, designed to offer quality instruction, terrific songs, and professional-quality audio with tons of full-demo tracks and instruction. Each book includes over 70 great songs and examples!

Play Accordion Today!
00701744	Level 1 Book/Audio	$10.99
00702657	Level 1 Songbook Book/Audio	$12.99

Play Alto Sax Today!
00842049	Level 1 Book/Audio	$9.99
00842050	Level 2 Book/Audio	$9.99
00320359	DVD	$14.95
00842051	Songbook Book/Audio	$12.95
00699555	Beginner's – Level 1 Book/Audio & DVD	$19.95
00699492	Play Today Plus Book/Audio	$14.95

Play Banjo Today!
00699897	Level 1 Book/Audio	$9.99
00701006	Level 2 Book/Audio	$9.99
00320913	DVD	$14.99
00115999	Songbook Book/Audio	$12.99
00701873	Beginner's – Level 1 Book/Audio & DVD	$19.95

Play Bass Today!
00842020	Level 1 Book/Audio	$9.99
00842036	Level 2 Book/Audio	$9.99
00320356	DVD	$14.95
00842037	Songbook Book/Audio	$12.95
00699552	Beginner's – Level 1 Book/Audio & DVD	$19.99

Play Cello Today!
00151353	Level 1 Book/Audio	$9.99

Play Clarinet Today!
00842046	Level 1 Book/Audio	$9.99
00842047	Level 2 Book/Audio	$9.99
00320358	DVD	$14.95
00842048	Songbook Book/Audio	$12.95
00699554	Beginner's – Level 1 Book/Audio & DVD	$19.95
00699490	Play Today Plus Book/Audio	$14.95

Play Dobro Today!
00701505	Level 1 Book/Audio	$9.99

Play Drums Today!
00842021	Level 1 Book/Audio	$9.99
00842038	Level 2 Book/Audio	$9.95
00320355	DVD	$14.95
00842039	Songbook Book/Audio	$12.95
00699551	Beginner's – Level 1 Book/Audio & DVD	$19.95
00703291	Starter	$24.99

Play Flute Today
00842043	Level 1 Book/Audio	$9.95
00842044	Level 2 Book/Audio	$9.99
00320360	DVD	$14.95
00842045	Songbook Book/Audio	$12.95
00699553	Beginner's – Level 1 Book/Audio & DVD	$19.95

Play Guitar Today!
00696100	Level 1 Book/Audio	$9.99
00696101	Level 2 Book/Audio	$9.99
00320353	DVD	$14.95
00696102	Songbook Book/Audio	$12.99
00699544	Beginner's – Level 1 Book/Audio & DVD	$19.95
00702431	Worship Songbook Book/Audio	$12.99
00695662	Complete Kit	$29.95

Play Harmonica Today!
00700179	Level 1 Book/Audio	$9.99
00320653	DVD	$14.99
00701875	Beginner's – Level 1 Book/Audio & DVD	$19.95

Play Mandolin Today!
00699911	Level 1 Book/Audio	$9.99
00320909	DVD	$14.99
00115029	Songbook Book/Audio	$12.99
00701874	Beginner's – Level 1 Book/Audio & DVD	$19.99

Play Piano Today!
Revised Edition
00842019	Level 1 Book/Audio	$9.99
00298773	Level 2 Book/Audio	$9.95
00842041	Songbook Book/Audio	$12.95
00699545	Beginner's – Level 1 Book/Audio & DVD	$19.95
00702415	Worship Songbook Book/Audio	$12.99
00703707	Complete Kit	$22.99

Play Recorder Today!
00700919	Level 1 Book/Audio	$7.99
00119830	Complete Kit	$19.99

Sing Today!
00699761	Level 1 Book/Audio	$10.99

Play Trombone Today!
00699917	Level 1 Book/Audio	$12.99
00320508	DVD	$14.95

Play Trumpet Today!
00842052	Level 1 Book/Audio	$9.99
00842053	Level 2 Book/Audio	$9.95
00320357	DVD	$14.95
00842054	Songbook Book/Audio	$12.95
00699556	Beginner's – Level 1 Book/Audio & DVD	$19.95

Play Ukulele Today!
00699638	Level 1 Book/Audio	$10.99
00699655	Play Today Plus Book/Audio	$9.99
00320985	DVD	$14.99
00701872	Beginner's – Level 1 Book/Audio & DVD	$19.95
00650743	Book/Audio/DVD with Ukulele	$39.99
00701002	Level 2 Book/Audio	$9.99
00702484	Level 2 Songbook Book/Audio	$12.99
00703290	Starter	$24.99

Play Viola Today!
00142679	Level 1 Book/Audio	$9.99

Play Violin Today!
00699748	Level 1 Book/Audio	$9.99
00701320	Level 2 Book/Audio	$9.99
00321076	DVD	$14.99
00701700	Songbook Book/Audio	$12.99
00701876	Beginner's – Level 1 Book/Audio & DVD	$19.95

HAL•LEONARD®

www.halleonard.com

HAL•LEONARD® SAXOPHONE PLAY-ALONG

The Saxophone Play-Along Series will help you play your favorite songs quickly and easily. Just follow the music, listen to the audio to hear how the saxophone should sound, and then play along using the separate backing tracks. Each song is printed twice in the book: once for alto and once for tenor saxes. The online audio is available for streaming or download using the unique code printed inside the book, and it includes **PLAYBACK+** options such as looping and tempo adjustments.

1. ROCK 'N' ROLL

Bony Moronie • Charlie Brown • Hand Clappin' • Honky Tonk (Parts 1 & 2) • I'm Walkin' • Lucille (You Won't Do Your Daddy's Will) • See You Later, Alligator • Shake, Rattle and Roll.

00113137 Book/Online Audio $16.99

2. R&B

Cleo's Mood • I Got a Woman • Pick up the Pieces • Respect • Shot Gun • Soul Finger • Soul Serenade • Unchain My Heart.

00113177 Book/Online Audio $16.99

3. CLASSIC ROCK

Baker Street • Deacon Blues • The Heart of Rock and Roll • Jazzman • Smooth Operator • Turn the Page • Who Can It Be Now? • Young Americans.

00113429 Book/Online Audio $16.99

4. SAX CLASSICS

Boulevard of Broken Dreams • Harlem Nocturne • Night Train • Peter Gunn • The Pink Panther • St. Thomas • Tequila • Yakety Sax.

00114393 Book/Online Audio. $16.99

5. CHARLIE PARKER

Billie's Bounce (Bill's Bounce) • Confirmation • Dewey Square • Donna Lee • Now's the Time • Ornithology • Scrapple from the Apple • Yardbird Suite.

00118286 Book/Online Audio $16.99

6. DAVE KOZ

All I See Is You • Can't Let You Go (The Sha La Song) • Emily • Honey-Dipped • Know You by Heart • Put the Top Down • Together Again • You Make Me Smile.

00118292 Book/Online Audio $16.99

7. GROVER WASHINGTON, JR.

East River Drive • Just the Two of Us • Let It Flow • Make Me a Memory (Sad Samba) • Mr. Magic • Take Five • Take Me There • Winelight.

00118293 Book/Online Audio $16.99

8. DAVID SANBORN

Anything You Want • Bang Bang • Chicago Song • Comin' Home Baby • The Dream • Hideaway • Slam • Straight to the Heart.

00125694 Book/Online Audio $16.99

9. CHRISTMAS

The Christmas Song (Chestnuts Roasting on an Open Fire) • Christmas Time Is Here • Count Your Blessings Instead of Sheep • Do You Hear What I Hear • Have Yourself a Merry Little Christmas • The Little Drummer Boy • White Christmas • Winter Wonderland.

00148170 Book/Online Audio $16.99

10. JOHN COLTRANE

Blue Train (Blue Trane) • Body and Soul • Central Park West • Cousin Mary • Giant Steps • Like Sonny (Simple Like) • My Favorite Things • Naima (Niema).

00193333 Book/Online Audio $16.99

11. JAZZ ICONS

Body and Soul • Con Alma • Oleo • Speak No Evil • Take Five • There Will Never Be Another You • Tune Up • Work Song.

00199296 Book/Online Audio $16.99

12. SMOOTH JAZZ

Bermuda Nights • Blue Water • Europa • Flirt • Love Is on the Way • Maputo • Songbird • Winelight.

00248670 Book/Online Audio $16.99

13. BONEY JAMES

Butter • Let It Go • Stone Groove • Stop, Look, Listen (To Your Heart) • Sweet Thing • Tick Tock • Total Experience • Vinyl.

00257186 Book/Online Audio $16.99

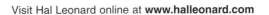

HAL•LEONARD®

Visit Hal Leonard online at **www.halleonard.com**

HAL•LEONARD INSTRUMENTAL PLAY-ALONG

Your favorite songs are arranged just for solo instrumentalists with this outstanding series. Each book includes great full-accompaniment play-along audio so you can sound just like a pro! Check out **www.halleonard.com** to see all the titles available.

The Beatles

All You Need Is Love • Blackbird • Day Tripper • Eleanor Rigby • Get Back • Here, There and Everywhere • Hey Jude • I Will • Let It Be • Lucy in the Sky with Diamonds • Ob-La-Di, Ob-La-Da • Penny Lane • Something • Ticket to Ride • Yesterday.

_____00225330 Flute $14.99
_____00225331 Clarinet $14.99
_____00225332 Alto Sax $14.99
_____00225333 Tenor Sax $14.99
_____00225334 Trumpet. $14.99
_____00225335 Horn $14.99
_____00225336 Trombone $14.99
_____00225337 Violin. $14.99
_____00225338 Viola $14.99
_____00225339 Cello $14.99

Chart Hits

All About That Bass • All of Me • Happy • Radioactive • Roar • Say Something • Shake It Off • A Sky Full of Stars • Someone like You • Stay with Me • Thinking Out Loud • Uptown Funk.

_____00146207 Flute $12.99
_____00146208 Clarinet $12.99
_____00146209 Alto Sax $12.99
_____00146210 Tenor Sax $12.99
_____00146211 Trumpet. $12.99
_____00146212 Horn $12.99
_____00146213 Trombone $12.99
_____00146214 Violin. $12.99
_____00146215 Viola $12.99
_____00146216 Cello $12.99

Disney Greats

Arabian Nights • Hawaiian Roller Coaster Ride • It's a Small World • Look Through My Eyes • Yo Ho (A Pirate's Life for Me) • and more.

_____00841934 Flute $12.99
_____00841935 Clarinet $12.99
_____00841936 Alto Sax $12.99
_____00841937 Tenor Sax $12.95
_____00841938 Trumpet. $12.99
_____00841939 Horn $12.99
_____00841940 Trombone $12.99
_____00841941 Violin. $12.99
_____00841942 Viola $12.99
_____00841943 Cello $12.99
_____00842078 Oboe $12.99

The Greatest Showman

Come Alive • From Now On • The Greatest Show • A Million Dreams • Never Enough • The Other Side • Rewrite the Stars • This Is Me • Tightrope.

_____00277389 Flute $14.99
_____00277390 Clarinet $14.99
_____00277391 Alto Sax $14.99
_____00277392 Tenor Sax $14.99
_____00277393 Trumpet. $14.99
_____00277394 Horn $14.99
_____00277395 Trombone $14.99
_____00277396 Violin. $14.99
_____00277397 Viola $14.99
_____00277398 Cello $14.99

Movie and TV Music

The Avengers • Doctor Who XI • Downton Abbey • Game of Thrones • Guardians of the Galaxy • Hawaii Five-O • Married Life • Rey's Theme (from *Star Wars: The Force Awakens*) • The X-Files • and more.

_____00261807 Flute $12.99
_____00261808 Clarinet $12.99
_____00261809 Alto Sax $12.99
_____00261810 Tenor Sax $12.99
_____00261811 Trumpet. $12.99
_____00261812 Horn $12.99
_____00261813 Trombone $12.99
_____00261814 Violin. $12.99
_____00261815 Viola $12.99
_____00261816 Cello $12.99

12 Pop Hits

Believer • Can't Stop the Feeling • Despacito • It Ain't Me • Look What You Made Me Do • Million Reasons • Perfect • Send My Love (To Your New Lover) • Shape of You • Slow Hands • Too Good at Goodbyes • What About Us.

_____00261790 Flute $12.99
_____00261791 Clarinet $12.99
_____00261792 Alto Sax $12.99
_____00261793 Tenor Sax $12.99
_____00261794 Trumpet. $12.99
_____00261795 Horn $12.99
_____00261796 Trombone $12.99
_____00261797 Violin. $12.99
_____00261798 Viola $12.99
_____00261799 Cello $12.99

Songs from Frozen, Tangled and Enchanted

Do You Want to Build a Snowman? • For the First Time in Forever • Happy Working Song • I See the Light • In Summer • Let It Go • Mother Knows Best • That's How You Know • True Love's First Kiss • When Will My Life Begin • and more.

_____00126921 Flute $14.99
_____00126922 Clarinet $14.99
_____00126923 Alto Sax $14.99
_____00126924 Tenor Sax $14.99
_____00126925 Trumpet. $14.99
_____00126926 Horn $14.99
_____00126927 Trombone $14.99
_____00126928 Violin. $14.99
_____00126929 Viola $14.99
_____00126930 Cello $14.99

Top Hits

Adventure of a Lifetime • Budapest • Die a Happy Man • Ex's & Oh's • Fight Song • Hello • Let It Go • Love Yourself • One Call Away • Pillowtalk • Stitches • Writing's on the Wall.

_____00171073 Flute $12.99
_____00171074 Clarinet $12.99
_____00171075 Alto Sax $12.99
_____00171106 Tenor Sax $12.99
_____00171107 Trumpet. $12.99
_____00171108 Horn $12.99
_____00171109 Trombone $12.99
_____00171110 Violin. $12.99
_____00171111 Viola $12.99
_____00171112 Cello $12.99

Wicked

As Long As You're Mine • Dancing Through Life • Defying Gravity • For Good • I'm Not That Girl • Popular • The Wizard and I • and more.

_____00842236 Flute $12.99
_____00842237 Clarinet $12.99
_____00842238 Alto Saxophone $12.99
_____00842239 Tenor Saxophone. $11.95
_____00842240 Trumpet. $12.99
_____00842241 Horn $12.99
_____00842242 Trombone $12.99
_____00842243 Violin. $12.99
_____00842244 Viola $12.99
_____00842245 Cello $12.99

Prices, contents, and availability subject to change without notice.
Disney characters and Artwork ™ & © 2018 Disney

HAL•LEONARD®

101 SONGS

BIG COLLECTIONS OF FAVORITE SONGS ARRANGED FOR SOLO INSTRUMENTALISTS.

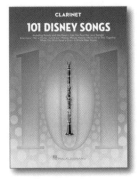

101 BROADWAY SONGS

00154199	Flute	$14.99
00154200	Clarinet	$14.99
00154201	Alto Sax	$14.99
00154202	Tenor Sax	$14.99
00154203	Trumpet	$14.99
00154204	Horn	$14.99
00154205	Trombone	$14.99
00154206	Violin	$14.99
00154207	Viola	$14.99
00154208	Cello	$14.99

101 HIT SONGS

00194561	Flute	$16.99
00197182	Clarinet	$16.99
00197183	Alto Sax	$16.99
00197184	Tenor Sax	$16.99
00197185	Trumpet	$16.99
00197186	Horn	$16.99
00197187	Trombone	$16.99
00197188	Violin	$16.99
00197189	Viola	$16.99
00197190	Cello	$16.99

101 CHRISTMAS SONGS

00278637	Flute	$14.99
00278638	Clarinet	$14.99
00278639	Alto Sax	$14.99
00278640	Tenor Sax	$14.99
00278641	Trumpet	$14.99
00278642	Horn	$14.99
00278643	Trombone	$14.99
00278644	Violin	$14.99
00278645	Viola	$14.99
00278646	Cello	$14.99

101 JAZZ SONGS

00146363	Flute	$14.99
00146364	Clarinet	$14.99
00146366	Alto Sax	$14.99
00146367	Tenor Sax	$14.99
00146368	Trumpet	$14.99
00146369	Horn	$14.99
00146370	Trombone	$14.99
00146371	Violin	$14.99
00146372	Viola	$14.99
00146373	Cello	$14.99

101 CLASSICAL THEMES

00155315	Flute	$14.99
00155317	Clarinet	$14.99
00155318	Alto Sax	$14.99
00155319	Tenor Sax	$14.99
00155320	Trumpet	$14.99
00155321	Horn	$14.99
00155322	Trombone	$14.99
00155323	Violin	$14.99
00155324	Viola	$14.99
00155325	Cello	$14.99

101 MOVIE HITS

00158087	Flute	$14.99
00158088	Clarinet	$14.99
00158089	Alto Sax	$14.99
00158090	Tenor Sax	$14.99
00158091	Trumpet	$14.99
00158092	Horn	$14.99
00158093	Trombone	$14.99
00158094	Violin	$14.99
00158095	Viola	$14.99
00158096	Cello	$14.99

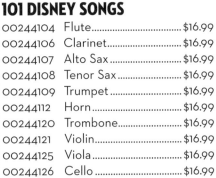

101 DISNEY SONGS

00244104	Flute	$16.99
00244106	Clarinet	$16.99
00244107	Alto Sax	$16.99
00244108	Tenor Sax	$16.99
00244109	Trumpet	$16.99
00244112	Horn	$16.99
00244120	Trombone	$16.99
00244121	Violin	$16.99
00244125	Viola	$16.99
00244126	Cello	$16.99

101 POPULAR SONGS

00224722	Flute	$16.99
00224723	Clarinet	$16.99
00224724	Alto Sax	$16.99
00224725	Tenor Sax	$16.99
00224726	Trumpet	$16.99
00224727	Horn	$16.99
00224728	Trombone	$16.99
00224729	Violin	$16.99
00224730	Viola	$16.99
00224731	Cello	$16.99

HAL•LEONARD®
www.halleonard.com

Prices, contents and availability subject to change without notice.